WILD BIRDS OF PREY!

HAWKS

By Deborah Kops

BLACKBIRCH PRESS, INC.
WOODBRIDGE, CONNECTICUT

Published by Blackbirch Press, Inc.
260 Amity Road
Woodbridge, CT 06525

Email: staff@blackbirch.com
Web site: www.blackbirch.com

©2000 by Blackbirch Press, Inc.
First Edition

Printed in the United States

10 9 8 7 6 5 4 3 2 1

Photo Credits: Cover: ©Corel Corporation; pages 4, 18, 22: Christopher Crowley/Cornell Ornithology; pages 5, 6, 9 (top & middle), 10, 11,12 (right), 14, 16 (right): ©Corel Corporation; pages 7, 8 (right), 12 (left), 13, 15: ©Rick Kline/Cornell Ornithology; page 8 (left): ©Frank Scheiler/Cornell Ornithology; page 9 (top): ©L. Page Brown/Cornell Ornithology; pages 14 (inset), 20, 21 (bottom): ©Isidor Jeklin/Cornell Ornithology; page 16: ©D. & E. Phillips/Cornell Ornithology; page 17: Scott Kamber/Cornell Ornithology; page 19: ©Joe Platt/Cornell Ornithology; page 21 (top): Mike Hopiak/Cornell Ornithology.

Library of Congress Cataloging-in-Publication Data
Kops, Deborah.
Hawks / By Deborah Kops
      p.   cm. — (Wild Birds of Prey!)
   Includes bibliographical references (p.) and index.
   Summary: Examines the special features and hunting behavior of hawks and describes the four main groups in North America: bird hawks, soaring hawks, kites and harriers.
   ISBN 1-56711-271-4
   1. Hawks— Juvenile literature. [1. Hawks.] I. Title. II. Series
QL696.F32 K69   2000
598.9'44 21—dc21

                                                              99-041620
                                                                     CIP

Dedication
For Noah

–DK

Contents

Introduction

The next time you're in the countryside, keep your eyes on the sky. You just might see a red-tailed hawk soaring in circles, high above a road or field. It will probably appear to be gliding—it won't flap its wings because it will most likely be riding in a thermal. A thermal is a column of rising warm air that lifts and transports a flier. You may also be able to see the outline of the hawk's primary feathers. They will be spread out at the ends of its wings like fingers.

Many species of hawks can be found in North America.

Hawks are in a family of birds called raptors, or birds of prey. This group also includes falcons, owls, osprey, eagles, and vultures. Like most birds, raptors eat other animals. These excellent hunters are among the best in the bird world.

Raptors are well equipped for hunting, regardless of their size. From the 11-inch-(28 centimeter) tall sharp-shinned hawk to a bald eagle almost 3 times its size, these birds share many special features. Raptors have long, curved claws called talons, which they use for grabbing and killing prey. They also have sharp, hooked beaks that tear captured prey. There are 58 different species, or kinds, of raptors in North America. More than a third of them are hawks.

Members of the Family

Cooper's hawks are medium-sized bird hawks.

North American hawks fall into 4 main groups: bird hawks, soaring hawks, kites, and harriers.

Bird Hawks

These birds get their name because they mainly hunt other birds. Bird hawks have short, rounded wings and long tails. Most species live in warm locations, but 3 types of bird hawks live in North America.

Cooper's hawks are medium-sized, gray-and-rust-colored birds. They live year-round in open woods, on farms, and in some suburbs. A sharp-shinned hawk looks like a small Cooper's hawk. It often keeps itself well hidden among trees.

The largest North American bird hawk is the northern goshawk. It is a large and powerful hunter. To catch its prey, this 2-foot- (61 centimeter) tall bird can fly at high speeds through the woods. Goshawks live year-round in northern woods and in mountain forests in the West. But about every 10 years, when their food supply is low, thousands of them migrate south for the winter in search of prey.

Northern goshawks are the largest North American bird hawks. They are also fierce and powerful hunters.

Kettles of Migrating Hawks

Each fall, migratory hawks travel from their breeding grounds to their winter homes to find food. To conserve their energy, hawks will fly in thermals. A hawk stays in a thermal and soars upward in spirals with the rising air. When it reaches the top height, it glides "downhill" to the next thermal. A huge flock of hawks will often enter the same thermal, bubbling up together like steam from a tea kettle. That's why a flock of hawks is called a "kettle."

Ferruginous hawks are the largest soaring hawks.

Soaring Hawks

North America's 15 species of soaring hawks have broad wings and short, wide tails. These birds seem to be built for gliding and soaring in open country, where most of them live. The most common species is the 19-inch- (48 centimeter) long red-tailed hawk. This hawk is a permanent resident of the United States. The largest soaring hawk is the ferruginous hawk. It nests in the dry plains, grasslands, and high deserts in the West. This eagle-like hawk has a very large wingspan. Measured from the tip of one wing to the tip of the other, it's about 4.5 feet (1.4 meters) wide!

Kites

Kites are a group of slender hawks that live all over the world. Most of them are very graceful fliers, which is why paper kites were named after them. There are 5 species of kites in North America. The hook-billed kite and the snail kite have paddle-shaped wings. The other 3 have pointed wings, including the beautiful swallow-tailed kite. This black-and-white bird soars and swoops effortlessly. Swallow-tails nest in Florida swamps and migrate farther south in the fall.

Harriers

The only harrier that lives in North America is the northern harrier. This long, slim hawk has a round facial disk that makes it look like an owl. Northern harriers live in the marshes and fields of Canada and the United States. Those birds that live in the northern part of their range migrate to southern states for the winter.

Top: Kites are graceful fliers.
Middle: White-tailed kites are 1 of 5 North American species.
Bottom: Northern harriers are the only harriers found in North America.

The Body of a Hawk

Hawk bodies vary a great deal in size, shape, and weight. A small sharp-shinned hawk can weigh as little as 3 ounces (85 grams). A large ferruginous hawk can weigh 4.5 pounds (2 kilograms). Like most raptors, female hawks are larger than males. This is unusual in the bird world. For instance, the 33-inch (84 centimeter) wingspan of a female Cooper's hawk is 4 inches (10 centimeters) longer than a male's. The female is also about 7 ounces (199 grams) heavier.

Another unusual raptor trait is their change in eye color as they become adults. A bird hawk's eyes, for example, start out gray and become a brilliant yellow, orange, or red.

Most hawks have a protective, bony ridge above their eyes. This ridge shields a hawk's eyes from the sun, and from getting scratched by tree branches. It also gives a hawk its fierce look.

Top: Most hawks have a bony ridge above their eyes for protection. **Bottom:** Sharp beaks and strong wings make hawks dangerous predators.

Compared to their bird relatives, hawks are not very colorful. Most of them are a combination of brown, gray, and white. This coloring camouflages them, making it more difficult for their prey to see them. Young hawks often have less noticeable markings than adults. Immature red-tails, for example, have not yet grown the brick-red tail feathers for which these birds are named.

Most hawks are not brightly colored, which is best for camouflage.

Special Features

A bird hawk's short, rounded wings and long tail allow it to fly quickly but quietly through thick woods to surprise prey. Its long, thin toes and sharp talons are ideal for grabbing and carrying birds. Soaring hawks have thicker legs and talons, and shorter toes. Their feet are better for holding small mammals and reptiles—their preferred prey.

Left: Long tails and thickly feathered wings allow bird hawks to fly silently while hunting prey.
Below: Long toes and sharp talons help hawks to grip and hold their prey.

A Day in the Life of a Hawk

Bird hawks seem to like to stretch their wings in the morning. They usually start the day soaring out in the open before they retreat into the woods.

A hawk spends most of its time on a perch, which is often a tree branch high above ground. From there, it can look out for a passing meal, or preen (groom) its feathers. The hawk gently pulls a feather through its partly closed beak or nibbles at it to remove dirt. If a hawk can find some shallow water, it will also take a bath. At the end of the day, it goes to its roost, which is a sheltered perch on which it sleeps.

Although they have a good sense of hearing, most hawks use only their eyes to find their prey. Along with eagles, these birds may have the sharpest vision of all raptors. They can see very small details at great distances. This is partly due to the large number of light-sensitive cells at the backs of their eyes. These cells help birds to see movement that humans cannot detect.

Northern harriers are unusual because they are one of the few raptors to use their sense of hearing when they hunt. Their owl-like facial disks reflect sounds back to their ears, increasing their ability to hear prey.

Hunting

Bird hawks and soaring hawks have different strengths and use different hunting techniques. Bird hawks are very good at ambushing prey. A Cooper's hawk may move quietly from one tree branch to the next, and then fly out suddenly to grab prey on the ground or in the air.

A soaring hawk sometimes flies a few hundred feet over open land to look for prey. When it spots a meal, it dives down at lightning speed and goes for the kill. This is a favorite technique of the slender Swainson's hawk.

Red-tailed hawks, like most soaring hawks, will dive and grab their prey with lightning speed.
Inset: Swainson's hawk.

A soaring hawk may also hunt from a perch, as red-shouldered hawks and red-tailed hawks usually do. Some soaring hawks look for prey that has been disturbed. In the West, white-tailed hawks gather at prairie fires, flying right through the smoke to chase fleeing snakes and lizards. Swainson's hawks are known to follow tractors in hopes of catching frightened mice or grasshoppers.

A northern harrier flies very low across a field, listening for the sounds of mice and birds.

The chestnut-and-gray Harris's hawk hunts in family groups. About 5 adults and offspring will chase prey until it is exhausted. When they share their kill, adults let the young eat first.

Harris's hawks often hunt in groups.

15

The Food Supply

Although bird hawks mainly eat birds, they consume other kinds of prey, too. Northern goshawks, for example, will also include rabbits and squirrels in their diets.

Soaring hawks prey on a variety of small mammals, reptiles, and rodents. Occasionally, they also catch birds. Red-tails are known for their flexible diets. They eat rabbits and squirrels when available, but they will also hunt snakes, frogs, and pigeons.

Left: A red-tailed hawk guards its prey.
Below: A sharp-shinned hawk stands over its prey.

A ferruginous hawk returns to her nest with a small rodent for her young to eat.

Most hawks like to eat on high perchs because they are safer from ground predators, such as coyotes. You can easily identify a bird hawk's favorite dining perch because the ground below is marked with a "feather doughnut." That's a ring of feathers it has plucked from its prey.

Mating and Nesting

Hawks begin their nesting season with thrilling courtship displays. These are performances that are meant to attract a mate and warn other birds away from their nesting territory. During a display, hawks will often fly up and dive repeatedly. Red-tailed hawks and white-tailed kites sometimes lock talons and cartwheel through the air.

Hawk nests need to be strong and long-lasting. Hawks will usually build nests out of sticks, high in a tree.

Red-shouldered hawks, like this male and female, may remain a pair for life.

They pick a spot that will give them good views of approaching predators. The nest has to be an easy place for parents to land with prey, and it has to be large enough so their young will have room to stretch their wings.

A Cooper's hawk mother guards her eggs.

When many bison, or buffalo, roamed in the western plains, ferruginous hawks built their nests out of bison bones. Today, they generally use sticks. Like many other hawks, a ferruginous pair often re-uses the same nest. Each year, they will add to it and make it stronger. Eventually a hawk nest may measure 3.5 feet (1 meter) across.

Each nesting season, a female hawk usually lays 2 to 4 eggs, called a clutch. She sits on the eggs to keep them warm for 30 to 35 days. Occasionally, she will share the work with her mate. This process is called incubation.

Raising Young

After hawk chicks hatch, the female stays with them while the male hunts. Northern harriers have a great system for delivering prey to the nest. When a female sees her mate returning from hunting, she flies up from the nest. Then she flips on her back, and catches the prey in the air! Like most female hawks, she will tear up the meat and feed it to her young (also called eyas). Providing food for chicks keeps hawk parents very busy. Many young hawks can eat about a pound of food each day!

Northern harrier chicks watch eagerly as their mother returns to the nest with food.

The young remain in the nest for 5 or 6 weeks. By then, their down (soft, early feathers) has been replaced by flight feathers, and they are ready to fledge (take their first flight). They stay near their parents for several weeks or more, until they can catch their own food.

Learning to fly, find food, and avoid enemies is difficult for a young hawk. If it survives its first year, a small sharp-shin lives about 5 years. A red-tail may survive for about 20.

Top: Broad-winged hawk chicks.
Bottom: A sharp-shinned hawk with her young.

Hawks and Humans

Humans have reduced the population of many hawk species by destroying their habitats. In the 1800s, forests were cleared to make room for farmland. This severely limited the territory of northern goshawks and they declined in number. More recently, retirement communities in Florida have replaced many of the marshes where gray-colored snail kites hunted for apple snails.

Red-shouldered hawks, like many North American birds, have had their habitats reduced by human activity.

In the West, ferruginous hawks have had their territories overrun by large herds of cattle on ranches.

All over North America, suburbs are expanding into undeveloped land. As a result, the woods and prairies that are closest to cities are disappearing. Not all hawk species are as adaptable as red-tails, which have adjusted to suburban

Red-tailed hawks have been able to adapt to changing conditions.

habitats and even live in cities. (One famous pair nests on an apartment building on Fifth Avenue, across from New York City's Central Park!)

People who are concerned about hawks and other wildlife have worked to set aside conservation land. The land is protected by law and cannot be developed into buildings or parking lots. Many suburban communities have also established conservation land in their towns. In many major cities, citizens protect large woodland treasures, such as Central Park, from ever being developed. Although people are the greatest threats to hawks, they are also their greatest hope for survival.

Glossary

game bird A bird that people hunt for food or for sport, such as a pheasant or grouse.

habitat A place where an animal lives, such as a rain forest or marsh.

migrate In this book, to move between a winter home and a nesting territory.

roost A place where a bird rests, or the action of resting.

thermal A column of rising warm air.

For More Information

Books

Arnold, Caroline. Robert Kruidenier (Photographer). *Hawk Highway in the Sky: Watching Raptor Migration*. Orlando, FL: Gulliver Books, 1997.

Fourie, Denise. Frank Balthis (Photographer). *Hawks, Owls, and Other Birds of Prey* (Close Up). Morristown, NJ: Silver Burdett Press, 1995.

Parry-Jones, Jemima. Mike Dunning (Photographer). *Amazing Birds of Prey*. New York, NY: Knopf, 1992.

Web Site

Birds of Prey
Find facts and photographs of many birds of prey—www.buteo.com

Index

24